MARTYN GOFF

The Royal Pavilion
Brighton

Folio Miniatures

MICHAEL JOSEPH
LONDON

FOLIO MINIATURES
General Editor: John Letts

First published in Great Britain by
Michael Joseph Ltd
52 Bedford Square
London WC1B 3EF
1976

© 1976 Martyn Goff

All Rights Reserved. No part of this
publication may be reproduced, stored in
a retrieval system, or transmitted in any
form or by any means, electronic, mechanical,
photocopying, recording or otherwise, without
the prior permission of the Copyright owner

ISBN 0 7181 1477 9

Endpaper: Nash's sectional view of the Royal Pavilion

PRINTED AND BOUND IN BELGIUM
by Henri Proost & Cie p.v.b.a., Turnhout

ACKNOWLEDGEMENTS
&
BIBLIOGRAPHY

Anyone writing about the Royal Pavilion is bound to be dependent on the standard work on the subject: *The Royal Pavilion* by Clifford Musgrave (1959). In addition the following proved helpful in illuminating particular aspects:

Papers of John Wilson Croker
(1884)
Correspondence of Princess Lieven & Lord Grey
(1890)
Brighton by Osbert Sitwell & Margaret Barton
(1935)
Princess Lieven: Private Letters by Peter Quennell
(1937)
Victoria R. I. by Elizabeth Longford
(1964)
Life in Brighton by Clifford Musgrave
(1970)
Talleyrand by J. F. Bernard
(1973)
George IV Regent & King by Christopher Hibbert
(1973)
George IV Prince of Wales by Christopher Hibbert
(1972)

Grateful acknowledgement is made to The Royal Pavilion for permission to reproduce all the pictures in this book, which include the Nash aquatints from his 'Views of the Royal Pavilion' and the colour photographs by Eric de Maré, except for the picture on page 4, which is by permission of the Victoria and Albert Museum, and those on pages 33 and 34 which are by permission of Angelo Hornak.

The Prince of Wales, later George IV, at the age of thirty-one; miniature by H. de Janvry, 1793.

I

The English middle classes have always oscillated between an admiration for puritan austerity and a love of eccentrics and eccentricities. The Royal Pavilion at Brighton in its final form, which is, on the outside at least, its present form, is just such an improbable eccentricity as captivates thousands while repelling other thousands. It is easy to sneer at the Taj Mahal as seen from a TV screen's distance; but if your first visit is by moonlight and there is a faint mist drifting through the minarets, then what you see is magic. Equally if your first sight of the Royal Pavilion is at night, the building floodlit in a delicate blue, puffs of sea mist gliding past the domes, then that too is magic. Nor is the magic all dissolved when next day you see Shah Jahan's monument or Nash's Royal Palace in the harsh light of the sun. *Magic* may be more elusive; they are still both incredibly beautiful buildings. Jahan's fantastic white marble mausoleum at Agra, dedicated to his wife's memory, started as that. Brighton's Royal Pavilion had much humbler origins: Henry Holland's original house on the site was completed in 1787. Forty-three years were to elapse before the same building officially became a Royal Palace.

We probably owe the arrival of George, Prince of Wales, in Brighton to two doctors who proclaimed the value of drinking(!) and immersing oneself in sea water as a cure for glandular diseases. The Prince had already visited Brighton in 1783, staying with his uncle, the Duke of Cumberland, in a house then known as Grove House. Ten months later the Prince paid a second visit, but this time he was preceded by Louis Weltje, Comptroller and Clerk to his Kitchens and Cellars, and a Mr Gill, Purveyor of his Stables. According to the *Sussex Weekly Advertiser* they had come 'to engage a house there for His Royal Highness, who had been advised by his physicians to sea-bathing as necessary to perfect the re-establishment of his health'. The Prince was then apparently suffering from swollen neck glands. His servants again took Grove House for him.

In 1786 Weltje found a farmhouse with a pleasant view of the seafront and leased it from Thomas Kemp, Member of Parliament for Lewes, a builder whose name was later to be given to that part of Brighton east of the Steine. The Prince of Wales meanwhile had in 1784 fallen madly in love with a Mrs Maria Fitzherbert, a North country Roman Catholic who, at twenty-eight, had already been twice widowed. He had pursued her so persistently that she had fled to France for a year. He had even staged an attempted suicide to win her promise of marrying him. On her return they were secretly wed, so that when he took up residence in Kemp's house, Mrs Fitzherbert was duly installed in a small villa nearby. The latter house, much changed, is still there, ironically serving as the Y.M.C.A.!

Thomas Kemp leased his house to Weltje for three years at £150 per annum, which rent included some furniture and fixtures. There was also an option clause to purchase for the sum of £3,000. Weltje in turn let the house to the Prince, agreeing to rebuild and refurbish it and then charge his master a rent that took such improvements into account. The Prince was a great friend and supporter of the Whig leader, Charles James Fox. The latter introduced him to Henry Holland, a young architect who was married to the daughter of 'Capability Brown', the famous landscape gardener. Holland had been appointed architect for the rebuilding of the Prince of Wales's London house, Carlton House, so it was only logical that he was retained to rebuild Kemp's house too.

Holland had to use 150 workmen to transform the house into the Pavilion between April and July 1787. But the transformation was not into any version of the oriental Palace we now know. Rather it had some resemblance to Holland's own Chelsea house, *Sloane Place*. It had affinities with Adam's classical style, with a circular salon framed in Greek Ionic columns. It also had bow windows on both wings, and the

The Duke of Cumberland's house in Steine, 1779

influence of this was enormous: bow-fronted villas appeared soon after opposite the Pavilion and the fashion quickly spread to other seasides. Much of Holland's redesigned house had interiors in the French style, Weltje buying some pieces at Paris sales. The Royal Archives tell us that the total cost of building, including a house next door for Weltje himself, stables and a coach house, was £22,338 10s. 11d. (1794).

Despite the elegance of the rebuilt house, Clifford Musgrave quotes the *New Brighton Guide* of 1796 saying:

> The Pavilion is built principally of wood; it is a nondescript monster in building, and appears like a mad house, or a house run mad, as it has neither beginning middle or end . . . The room in which the Prince usually dines may be compared to a sort of oven: when the fire is lighted the inmates are nearly baked or incrusted.

But Musgrave also cites a letter written some years earlier which gives us a contrary viewpoint while painting an intriguing picture of the Prince:

> We have had frequent views of His Royal Highness and Mrs Fitzherbert, the Duke and Dutchess of Cumberland, Lady Elizth lately the Princess Elizabeth, last Night they were walking on the Stein, the P— between the Dutchess and Mrs F—. Each had hold of one arm, and in that manner went tugging him along; his new house is very handsome, a grand Dome in the Centre, with Wings, and and a good deal of ground before with a Ha! Ha!* and behind is a noble square, with Pillars and Lamps between...

Whichever view one took of the Marine Pavilion, it remained true that by 1794 the Prince of Wales was £640,000 in debt. If King George III, his father, were to bail him out, then the price was marriage. The Prince, who had already transferred his affection from Mrs Fitzherbert to Lady Jersey, gave in ungraciously: 'One damned Frau is as good as another', he answered when told that his wife was to be Princess Caroline of Brunswick. Although a child, Princess Charlotte, was born at the beginning of 1796, the couple lived apart after her birth and the Prince a little later swung back from Lady Jersey to Mrs Fitzherbert.

*A sunken fence placed in a ditch to provide a barrier without marring the view.

The Saloon at the Royal Pavilion, by Thomas Rowlandson

This reunion was celebrated by the return of the Prince's Court to Brighton and the next stage in the transformation of the Pavilion. Henry Holland being in Cornwall at the time, the designs were prepared by P. F. Robinson, his assistant, later to become famous as the architect of the 'Swiss Cottage' in Hampstead. While the exterior changes resulted largely in making the building look less grand, partly by the addition of shell-like canopies over the windows and long, trellised verandahs, the interior was totally transformed into a Chinese fantasy.

In *Illustrations of His Majesty's Palace at Brighton: formerly the Pavilion* (published in 1838) Edward Brayley tells us how the walls were hung with several pieces of a very beautiful Chinese paper that had been given to the Prince in 1802:

> Other parts of the Gallery were painted and decorated in a corresponding style. About the same time, the

passage room was constructed in a singular manner. A space was enclosed within it, measuring twelve feet by eight, the sides and upper part of which were entirely formed of stained glass, of an oriental character, and exhibiting the peculiar insects, fruit, flowers, etc. of China. It was illuminated from without; and through it, as through an immense Chinese lantern, the communication was carried on: its effect is stated to have been extremely beautiful.

The accounts of Crace and Sons, through whom the Prince bought lacquer cabinets, bamboo stools and chairs and Chinese porcelain, show that most of the items had been imported. There were even model pagodas, costumes, birds nests and a Chinese razor. The Countess of Bessborough had had no idea that 'strange Chinese shapes and columns could have looked so well'. Mary Berry disagreed: 'it was more like a china shop . . . than the abode of a Prince.' Whatever the differences of opinion over the decoration, life at the Pavilion in 1805 seemed to be very pleasant. Lady Bessborough in a letter to Lord Granville Leveson Gower wrote:

[The Prince's] way of living is pleasant enough, especially if one might chuse one's society. In the Morning he gives you horses, Carriages, etc., to go where you please with you; he comes and sits *rather too long*, but only on a visit. Everbody meets at dinner, which *par parenthèse*, is excellent, with the additions of a few invitations in the evening. Three large rooms, very comfortable, are lit up; whist, backgammon, Chess, trace Madame – every sort of game you can think of in two of them, and Musick in the third. His band is beautiful. He has Viotti and a Lady who sings and plays very well. A few people have the entree and a few more are invited. Mrs Fitzherbert is ill at present and confined to her bed, so he makes me do the honours.

Similarly in the Creevey papers we learn that the Prince at this time 'was always merry and full of his jokes, and any one would have said he was a really happy man'.

The Prince had earlier had the idea of altering the outside in the Chinese style; both Holland in 1801 and Porden, his successor, in 1805, had made sketches accordingly. Porden's master, Samuel Pepys Cockerell, had designed Sezincote, a large house in Gloucestershire, in the Indian style. This took the Prince's fancy. Humphrey Repton, who was responsible for Sezincote's gardens, was asked to suggest 'the style of architecture most suitable for the Pavilion'. By 1807 he had made designs for an Indian building. The Prince was delighted but too short of money to go ahead.

So instead he ordered the building of an immense stables and riding house in the Pavilion's grounds. While the Prince was inspecting this Indian edifice when it was still under construction, he announced that he was so pleased with it that 'he should like to have a Palace on the same plan, the central area to be a vast hall of accomodation to the apartments ranged around, with four staircases'. This move from Chinese to Indian influence reflected a more general one, as we can see in the work of Southey, Byron and Shelley (Byron had visited the Prince in 1808 and 1812), while painters like Hodges and the Daniells were bringing back paintings underscoring the romance and strangeness of the great continent.

The central cupola of the new building, now the Dome Concert Hall, was over 85 feet wide and 65 feet high. The frame held huge leaf-shaped glass panels with gilded leaves forming the ventilating lantern. The Riding House, now the Corn Exchange, was 178 feet long and 58 feet wide. The Dome, Riding House, harnessing rooms and the adjoining accommodation for ostlers and grooms cost £55,000 and took three years to build. This was partly because of the French blockade of Baltic ports, making it difficult to get timber long enough for the vast dome, and partly because the Prince did not have enough money to pay the workmen. The architect complained that he was 'harrassed with letters from the tradesmen at Brighton. The distress of many of these creditors is I believe very great and the clamour against his Royal Highness will be in proportion.' It was the same architect, William Porden, who had built Mrs Fitzherbert's new house on the Steine for £6,300.

In 1807 the Prince was at last able to buy the Pavilion for the sum of £17,000. Louis Weltje had died in 1800, but his widow received an annuity of £360 as part of the deal. Not altogether surprisingly the Prince raised a mortgage on the property, this from Louis Weltje's brother, Christopher. The interest was £850 per annum. But his plans for an Indian Pavilion got no farther than Repton's designs, for which he was paid £713 15s. 6d. The architect published them in 1808 as *Designs for the Pavilion at Brighton*, naturally hoping that when the Prince finally was in sufficient funds to carry them out, he would be given the job. Had not H.R.H. himself written:

> Mr Repton, I consider the whole of the work as perfect, and will have my part carried into immediate execution; not a tittle shall be altered – even you yourself shall not admit any improvement.

But in 1812 it was James Wyatt, then at the height of his fame as the architect of Ashridge and Heveningham, who was given the commission. And when he was killed in September 1813 in a carriage accident, the chance passed to John Nash.

II

Nash received his commission in January 1815 from Sir Benjamin Bloomfield, the Prince's Private Secretary. More than ten years later the great architect produced a book called *View of the Royal Pavilion*. For this he wrote a long preface which was never published but which found its way into the Royal Archives. Having given a brief history of the Pavilion to date, Nash continues:

> H.M. disliked the oblique position of the dining-room and Conservatory and the latter was found to be entirely useless. H.M. was also offended with the incongruity of character between the Stables and the Pavilion and with the comparatively mean appearance of the latter, but it became a subject of serious consideration whether the intended alteration of the Pavilion should assume an Eastern character in conformity with that of the Stables or retain its modern character and the Stables be planted out or its Eastern character obliterated . . . It was therefore determined by HM that the Pavilion should assume an Eastern character, and the Hindoo style of Architecture was adopted in the expectation that the turban domes and lofty pinnacles might, from their glittering and picturesque effect, attract and fix the attention of the Spectator, and the superior magnitude of the Dome and the Stables cease to be observed.

While inspiration came from the East, a local addition was cast iron. This was used for the staircases at either end of the new Gallery, being worked into imitation bamboo. It was also used for the framework of the domes and the bases of the chimneys and pinnacles. Finally the columns in the Kitchen were made of cast iron, while the leaves of the palm trees at their tops supporting the ceiling were made from copper.

The work proceeded slowly, too slowly indeed for the Prince. As early as the summer of 1815 he was expressing his great annoyance at the lack of progress in the work. The workmen were encouraged to labour at night and on Sundays by double and even treble pay. Nor did the Prince help matters. Between July and December 1815, for example, the decorations in the south wing were changed four times!

When all the alterations had been completed, Nash had spent £148,000. The Prince, who had become Prince Regent in February 1811, was visited by his mother, Queen Charlotte, in 1817. She was so pleased with the new look of the Pavilion that she made the Prince a grant of £50,000 towards the improvements 'from her private purse'. Even with this help, the Prince was still sufficiently appalled by the cost of the work he had ordered to blame Nash for overspending. When George ascended the throne on the death of his father, George III, at the beginning of 1820, Nash wrote to his Private Secretary:

> How then and in what can I be blamed and how have I lost the countenance of the King? I am anxious that the work has been done at the least possible expense.

Shortly after, in another letter, Nash goes on:

> I will not aggravate your feelings by arguments in justic^n of myself – though much very much should be taken into consideration – that passage in your Letter when you said you had a pride in saying to thousands that so gigantic a work had been done within my estimate – I have but one thing in my power in regard to the Accounts. I have not, nor will I charge the King anything for myself.

Two years later, however, Sir William Knighton, Bloomfield's successor as Private Secretary, wrote:

> I am very happy and *much satisfied* that Mr Nash's account is brought to a close . . . I think it will be right to allow him his commission.

Eventually Nash was paid £4,646 13s. 10d. which even then was much less than the £7,800 he had been willing to forgo in the earlier letter quoted.

Neither as Prince nor King had George lacked warnings about his extravagance. In March 1816, for example, he had had one jointly signed by the Prime Minister, the Foreign Secretary and the Chancellor of the Exchequer. 'Your Royal Highness's servants', the letter ends

> humbly submit that the only means by which [there] can be a prospect of weathering the impending storm is by stating on the direct authority of your Royal Highness and by your command, if it should be necessary, that all new expenses for additions or alterations at Brighton or elsewhere will, under present circumstances, be abandoned. Your Royal Highness's servants are perfectly convinced that Parliament will never vote one shilling for defraying such expenses if unfortunately they were to be persevered in.

John Wilson Croker records in his *Journals* that he visited the Pavilion at the end of 1818. By then Nash's two great new rooms, the Music Room and the Banqueting Room, with their gigantic chandeliers and ornately painted domed ceilings, were both finished. While Croker thought them 'too handsome for Brighton' (!), he also thought that the outside had been 'copied from its own stables, which, perhaps, were borrowed from the Kremlin'. In any case, he went on, it was all 'an absurd waste of money' and would become 'a ruin in half a century or sooner'. Although, as we shall see, his prediction almost came true, what seemed monstrous extravagance on George IV's part at the time has become a small investment set against the pleasure which countless thousands have taken in the Royal Pavilion ever since.

The grand rooms were not all that Nash altered. There was also a splendid new Kitchen in 1817, looking much as it does today with 'such contrivances for roasting, boiling, baking, stewing, frying, steaming and heating; hot plates, hot closets,

The North Front of Nash's Pavilion, drawn by Pugin, 1822

hot air, and hot hearths, with all manner of cocks for hot water and cold water, and warm water and steam, and twenty saucepans all ticketed and labelled, placed up to their necks in a vapour bath', as we learn from Croker's journal of 1818.

In Roger Fulford's book *George IV* we learn that for a time the famous French chef, Antonin Carême, worked in the kitchen. On 15th January, 1817 he provided a menu of four soups, four different fish dishes and thirty-six entrées. A

detailed description of the first item will suffice to show just how elaborate the menu was:

Quatre Potages
Le Potage à la Monglas
La garbure aux chous
Le potage d'orge perlée à la Crecy
Le potage de poissons à la Russe

Not only were the menus formal and complex. The good Croker records in his *Journals* the procedure:

> The etiquette is, that before dinner when he comes in, he *finds* all the men standing, and the women rise; he speaks to everybody, shakes hands with new comers or particular friends, then desires the ladies to be seated. When dinner is announced, he leads out a lady of the highest rank or when the ranks are nearly equal, or when the nominal rank interferes a little with the real rank, as yesterday, with Lady Liddell and Mrs Pelham, he took one on each arm . . . The ceilings of both rooms are spherical and yet there is no echo. Nash says he has avoided it by some new theory of sound, which he endeavoured to explain, and which I did not understand, nor I believe in neither. The rooms are as full of lamps as Hancock's shop.

This was in 1818. For the next two years George had to make do with a nearby house while the decoration of the Palace dragged on.

The Russian Ambassador to England at this time was Prince Lieven. His wife was known for her wit, her charm and her good looks as well as for her malice. She was also known for fairly stupendous powers of exaggeration. She had lived in England since 1812 and knew almost everyone of power and influence in the country. Talleyrand's niece, the Duchess of Sagan, wrote that 'Madame de Lieven is the woman to be most feared, respected, cultivated and courted'. In 1819 and 1820 the Princess attended the Prince Regent's (by the latter date, the King's) Court in Brighton. To her friend Prince Metternich she wrote:

> In the middle of all this, the King occupies a little house two hundred yards from his palace, or pavilion, or kremlin, or mosque – for it bears all these names and deserves them – quite alone, without means of receiving anybody, since his lodging is no bigger than a parrot's cage.

In a later letter she added:

> I went with him [the Duke of York] again to see the work going on at the Kremlin. We were shown a chandelier which cost eleven thousand pounds sterling – I write it out in full because it is really incredible. The chandelier is in the form of a tulip held by a dragon. I send you a bad, but faithful, engraving of the King's Palace here. How can one describe such a piece of architecture? The style is a mixture of Moorish, Tartar, Gothic and Chinese, and all in stone and iron. It is a whim which has already cost £700,000; and is still not fit to live in.
>
> I do not believe that, since the days of Heliogabalus, there has been such magnificence and such luxury. There is something effeminate in it which is disgusting. One spends the evening half lying on cushions; the lights are dazzling; there are perfumes, music, liqueurs . . . Here is one single detail about the establishment. To light the three rooms, used when the family is alone, costs 150 guineas an evening; when the apartment is fully opened up, it is double that.

The cost of the lighting, even if exaggerated by the Princess, was only one among a number of extravagances. The King's Band in the early eighteen-twenties numbered seventy musicians, costing him some £7,000 per annum. On 29th December, 1823 a grand concert was held in the Music Room. The programme included Rossini's Overture to *The Thievish Magpie* and the great composer was there in person not only to conduct it, but also to sing two arias from his own operas.

Whatever George IV's pleasure in his new palace, his visits became fewer and fewer once the improvements were completed. Clifford Musgrave refutes the idea that the King had grown tired of Brighton. Certainly he became increasingly ill, and, at the same time, increasingly involved in the transformation of Windsor Castle.

The King's last visit to the Royal Pavilion started on 23rd January, 1827 and lasted until the end of the first week in

March. The *Brighton Herald* reflected the enthusiasm the much postponed visit created:

> At length we have the happiness to state – a feeling in which the whole town warmly participates, – that the King is again residing among us.

On 10th March, echoing the same feelings, the paper reported:

> We have this week the painful task of announcing the departure of the King for Windsor . . . A large concourse of the town's people assembled to bid adieu to their beloved Patron.

The term 'Patron' was indeed earned. Since the Prince's first visit in 1783 the town had grown enormously. During his period on the throne the number of houses nearly doubled, more than 500 being built in 1826 alone. The number of summer visitors began to reach five figures. The presence of the new Pavilion and the Court had much to do with the town's rapid growth. But there was a disadvantage in all this for the King himself. Much of the building initially took place round the Pavilion and so destroyed the privacy that the King so dearly valued in his last years. Just the same, when he finally died on 26th June, 1830, George IV had bequeathed a unique palace, a vision of his imagination and taste, to the town – and the nation.

The King's brother, who succeeded him as William IV, paid his first visit to Brighton two months later. The very next day he was seen with Nash in the grounds of the Pavilion, clearly discussing the building with its architect. Two weeks later the King was back, this time with his Queen. 500 schoolchildren and 75 sailors were waiting to greet them.

During their first visit the King invited Mrs Fitzherbert to dine. She declined because of 'the peculiar difficulties of her situation', so the King called on her in her own house instead. There she showed him the document which proved she had indeed been George IV's real wife. The King was so moved by this that he at once offered to make her a Duchess. But she refused. But she did come to the Pavilion soon after to dine:

> I was overwhelmed with kisses from male and female, the Princess was particularly gracious [Mrs Fitzherbert wrote in her letter]. I felt rather nervous, never having been in the Pavilion since I was drove away by Lady Hertford. I cannot tell you of my astonishment at the magnificence and the total change in that house since my first acquaintance with it. They lead a very quiet life – his family the only inhabitants. I think I counted eight Fitz Clarences.

Mrs Fitzherbert, who was then in her 75th year, continued to be a regular visitor to the Pavilion until her death in 1837.

In the following year William IV began to make a number of changes and additions in line with the intention to change the building from the Royal Pavilion to the Royal Palace. Although he had discussed it with Nash at the start of his reign, it was Joseph Good, Clerk of the Works to the Board of Ordnance, who actually designed and carried out the work. Extra accommodation for visitors came first, followed by a new arched gateway and South Lodge. The Stables were enlarged with the building that now forms the Art Gallery and Museum. Finally the North Lodge, now called North Gate, was erected from the original designs by Nash, though carried out by Good.

In 1833 the King and Queen came to Brighton in November and stayed for three months. For some years after that they came every winter, Queen Adelaide using the rooms above the King's Apartments. She is reputed to have dreamt that the great chandelier in the Banqueting Room had fallen and killed the King. Whether or not this was the reason, it was certainly taken down and stored until 1842. In other ways the splendour and formality was kept up. We learn from a contemporary diary that:

> The magnificence of the parties given by the King and

Queen at the Pavilion are spoken of as realising the ideas of the entertainments described in the 'Arabian Nights', the dinners consisting daily of about forty persons.

But by 1837 the King was dead. Four months after coming to the throne, Queen Victoria came to the Royal Pavilion on what was, surprisingly, her first visit ever to Brighton. She was greeted with even more panoply and ceremony than William IV, but this was not enough to reconcile her to the palace. 'The Pavilion is a strange, odd, Chinese-looking thing, both inside and outside, most rooms low,' she confided to her journal. 'I only see a little morsel of the sea from one of my sitting-room windows.' She came again in 1838 but four more years elapsed before her third visit.

Then in August 1843 she left the Princess Royal, the Prince of Wales and the Princess Alice at the Pavilion while she visited the French Emperor, Louis-Philippe. Returning to Brighton in the Royal Yacht, she was given a splendid welcome at the Chain Pier. This Pier, which had much in common with Telford's Menai Straits suspension bridge or Brunel's Clifton Bridge at Bristol, was built in 1823 by Samuel Brown (with the co-operation of Telford himself). Already in 1829 William IV, then still Duke of Clarence, had landed there in great style on his return from France. Although it was badly damaged by storms on a number of occasions, it was not finally washed away until 1896.

During her 1843 visit Queen Victoria used to like walking on the Pier as well as along the sea front itself. The Queen, however, found the general lack of privacy extremely trying. She wrote to her aunt a couple of years later, on what was to be her last stay in the Pavilion, that 'the people are very indiscreet and troublesome here really, which makes this place quite a prison'. *Punch* at that time also commented that 'Her Majesty and her Royal Consort cannot walk abroad like other people, without having a pack of ill-bred dogs at their heels, hunting them to the very gates of the Pavilion'. As a result the Royal Pavilion was to lose its royalty henceforth.

In 1850 the Keeper of Her Majesty's Purse noted that:

> The Queen shortly after the Marriage finding that the Pavilion was rendered useless to her as a marine residence, instead of applying to the Country for another Palace upon the coast, was enabled by economy to purchase for Herself a property upon the Seaside and to build upon it from her own funds a private residence [Osborne on the Isle of Wight, bought for £26,000]. The Queen did not receive the purchase money for which the Pavilion was sold to enable her to buy a Marine residence in its stead – that sum went to relieve the Country from the necessary improvements to Buckingham Palace. The Queen did not apply the decoration or furniture from the Pavilion to embellish Osborne – they were used to save the public the cost of furniture for the New Wing in Buckhm. Palace.

Brighton was not incorporated as a Borough until 1854. Until then it was run by 112 Town Commissioners whose Clerk was one Lewis Slight, a man of great drive and ability. As soon as rumours started spreading that the Pavilion was to be demolished, he resolved to acquire the building for the town. As a start in 1846 he persuaded the Town Commissioners to set up a committee 'to consider the proceedings to be taken, in order, if possible, to avoid the sale or disposal of the Pavilion at Brighton'.

Soon after, the dismantling of the Pavilion started. In 1847 and 1848 nearly 150 vanloads of furniture and carpets were taken from it and delivered to Windsor, Buckingham Palace and Kensington Palace. A public sale was held in the building itself; the servants were dismissed. On 6th June 1848 the great building was finally stripped and locked.

During the following year the Committee of Woods and Forests sponsored a Bill in the House of Commons allowing them to sell or otherwise dispose or pull down the same, and to sell the Materials thereof, and to sell demise or otherwise dispose of the land and hereditaments aforesaid comprising the site of the said Royal Pavilion and the lawns and grounds thereof and to apply the residue of all money received in and towards the expenses incurred or to be incurred of repairing, improving and enlarging Her Majesty's Palace called Buckingham Palace.

A petition to prevent the sale of the building – possibly to Cubitt for £100,000, that astute builder already having plans to put houses on the site – and signed by 7,406 people, led to a Select Committee being appointed. This Committee finally gave the town one month in which to make the purchase for £53,000. All was not yet clear sailing, since antipathy between Lewis Slight and some of the Town Commissioners led to the need for a referendum of the town's citizens. The vote was 1,343 to 1,307 in favour of the purchase.

The Bill authorising the sale was not passed until May 1850. The Bank of England lent Brighton £60,000 out of which £53,000 was handed to the Commissioners of Woods and Forests on June 18th. Next day their Surveyor formally transferred the Pavilion to Lewis Slight. But the men from Woods and Forests had not quite finished. *The New Monthly Magazine* reported:

> To get at the copper bell-wire, which was afterwards sold at the nearest marine store for threepence a pound, these devastators tore off the skirting boards in every apartment in the palace ... they shivered the household gods – the Chinese idols – wherever they were to be met with, either sculptured on pedestals or painted on the walls; the rare and curious paper, with all its emblems of the Celestial Empire, was torn into shreds; in short, if a pack of Kozacs from the Don, a band of Red Republicans from Paris, or a host of Californian gold-seekers had been turned loose into the Pavilion, with instructions, as the Americans say, to do their —— worst,

they could not have committed a tithe of the ravages effected by the delegates of the 'Woods and Forests' in simply *removing the fixtures*!

The citizens of Brighton were not, however, to be robbed of the pleasure of their purchase. Two months after its completion they spent £4,500 on putting ten of the rooms into reasonable order. Christopher Vick, who had worked on the Palace during William IV's reign, with the help of Lambelet, who originally had painted the wall paintings in the Music Room, carried out the redecoration with taste and skill. The original drawings for some of their work can still be seen in two watercolours now hanging in the Pavilion (see plate   ). One thousand, four hundred people attended a Grand Pavilion Ball on 21st January, 1851 to celebrate the refurbished apartments. Lewis Slight had an extra celebration of his own, having redone nineteen instead of the agreed ten rooms – at, needless to add, great extra cost!

By 1856 the Brighton Town Council had become not unreasonably concerned about the cost of keeping the Pavilion in good shape; and accordingly encouraged its use for public and private functions on an ever increasing scale. Even the great Kitchen had already, in 1852, been used for art exhibitions; while rooms on the first floor served as a museum and reference library until the Public Library and Art Gallery and Museum were opened in the former Queen Adelaide stables and coachhouses in 1873.

In 1852 Francis De Val was appointed Custodian of the Pavilion. He had known the palace in his youth when he had worked for a glass warehouse whose owner was the King's chief bandsman. De Val persuaded the Lord Chamberlain to allow him and the Borough Surveyor to inspect the remaining unpacked cases of Pavilion furniture and ornaments that were stored at Kensington Palace. Queen Victoria permitted the contents to be returned to Brighton with the result that back came the original Music Room wall paintings, some of the chandeliers, wallpapers, dragons, phoenixes and the like.

The real restoration had begun, and was entrusted to a Monsieur Tony Dury from Lyons.

Interior of the Dome in 1875, now a concert hall.

Despite the proud beginnings, the remainder of the century witnessed a strong downturn in the condition of the Pavilion. Colours were changed for the worse; paintings were over-painted instead of being restored. The white and gold of the South Drawing Room became dark brown; the palm-tree columns chocolate! The pink of the Long Gallery became dark red brown; the magical blue of the trees Victorian aspidistra green.

In 1914 the spirit of the place, if not the decoration, was uplifted when King George V's suggestion of turning the Pavilion into a hospital for Indian soldiers was accepted. This occupancy was commemorated by the people of India by giving the Pavilion a new South Gate in 1921. Though the Gate is strictly Indian, it differs in style from the Pavilion itself, which is rather a fantasy on Indian themes.

King George V also continued Queen Victoria's policy of returning to the Pavilion objets d'art, furniture and ornaments that had been removed in 1848. The eight splendid standard lamps from the Banqueting Room came back from Windsor Castle. Queen Mary bought and presented to the Pavilion a grand piano almost identical with the one that had stood in the North Drawing Room. The two pedestals now back in their original place in the Long Gallery were brought from Sandringham.

But the major step in restoring the Pavilion came with the foundation of the Regency Society of Brighton and Hove in 1945. This led to the Regency Exhibition of 1946, the main aim of which was to see the building furnished as it had once been. Furniture of the period was lent by a host of people including King George VI and Queen Elizabeth. The magnificent Aubusson circular carpet, said to have been designed for Tsarskoe Selo, was among them; and a fund was raised to purchase it for the Pavilion. A second Regency Exhibition was held two years later which proved to be even more splendid than the first.

The final steps in the complete restoration of the building were taken in 1949 when Brighton Borough Council decided to furnish the State Apartments as far as possible in the manner of George IV's time; and to open them to the public throughout the year. Meetings, entertainments and assemblies were sharply reduced, being confined from then on to cultural and civic events. On 9th June, 1950 the Duke and Duchess of Devonshire opened the Pavilion in its new state. This was not, in fact, the final peak. That occurred in 1965 when Queen Elizabeth II permanently loaned the Royal Pavilion over a hundred articles of the original furnishings from Buckingham Palace. These included Chinese bamboo chairs, lacquered cabinets of all sizes, cloisonné figures and lacquered boxes.

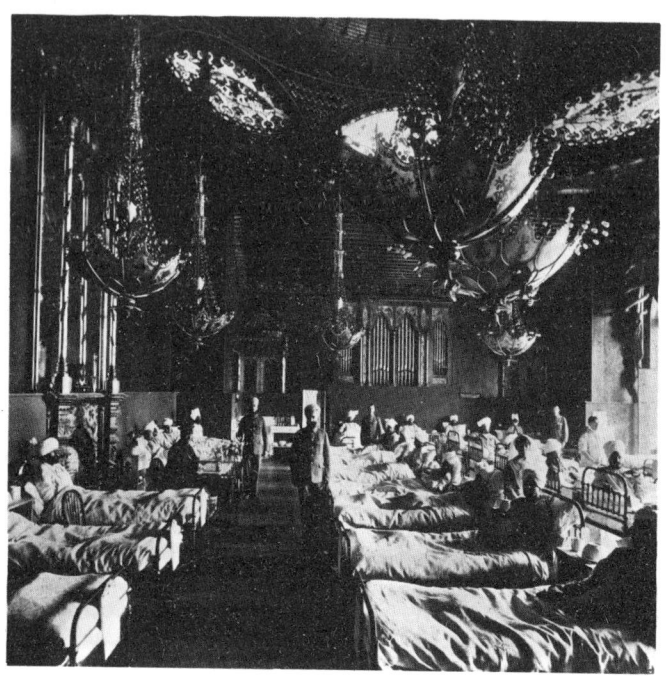

The Music Room in the Pavilion being used as an Indian Military Hospital, after 1914

The gifts had the further effect of stimulating the restoration of the Corridor as nearly as possible into its original form. Two years after, similar work was inaugurated on the Banqueting Room.

However much each step at the time seemed the last, restoration was even now not yet finished. In 1960 the Queen sent back four pedestal candelabra from Windsor; in 1966 George IV's Coronation robes were lent by Madame Tussaud's; and Buckingham Palace contributed on loan silver-gilt banqueting articles that had originally been bought by

George IV. More and more the Palace attained to the words of Sir Osbert Sitwell, written as far back as 1935:

> ... not even Windsor, although the work was conceived on so gigantic a scale, ranks as a higher achievement than the Pavilion; for to this singular dwelling undoubtedly attaches something of the dreamlike quality of great poetry.

III

And what does the contemporary visitor see on his first visit to the Royal Pavilion? First, one of the most fully and authentically restored Palaces in the world. Few other royal or formerly royal buildings can boast so complete a set of decorations and furnishings. Visitors in George IV's time entered by the Octagon Hall; visitors today do the same. The chairs are those that were there originally; the fireplace is as it was. Moving on into the Vestibule our visitor will find the same light green walls as he would have done in 1821.

Then suddenly he steps into the Corridor, once known as the Long Gallery. It had been intended to restore this in light pink, but when fragments of the original decorations were found unfaded under the mouldings, the present absolutely accurate pink was used. Painted in oil on cartridge paper spread on linen, the walls are decorated with blue foliage. To the Chinese lanterns and figures, banners and pennants, are added the furniture and staircases of bamboo. Only the staircases are made of cast iron and the chairs of wood fashioned to look like bamboo; the very same imitation bamboo that was in the Corridor in George IV's time.

From the Corridor our visitor moves into the Banqueting Room just as the King and his party had once done. Above the diners is a huge domed ceiling, forty-five feet high, and covered by a large plantain tree from which descends the celebrated gasolier. This central light alone weighs nearly a ton and is thirty feet high, surrounded by four smaller gasoliers each ten feet tall. On the west wall is a Chinese painting. Its dominating figure is supposed to represent Lady Conyngham, who succeeded Lady Hertford as the King's favourite in 1821.

The Banqueting Room was served from the Great Kitchen which, as we have seen, was marvellously equipped in 1816 and looks today much as it did then (see Plate 15). Returning on the east side of the Palace, our visitor now enters the South Drawing Room. Not only is this one of the most effective of all rooms but it is also a most welcoming one, a room that most people could imagine themselves living in even now without having to make too many changes. Once more decorations and furniture are as they were in 1821, faithful to the last of George IV's many colour schemes for the room.

The Saloon, next door, was once the original heart of the whole building. The mirrors and doors, the domed ceiling and pilasters are all original; only the fireplace is a later addition. So too are most of the decorations and contents in the North Drawing Room, a room that totally fails to prepare us for the fantastic and exotic Music Room beyond. Here are a ceiling surrounded by gilded cockleshells, dragons climbing columns, Yung Cheng pagodas, Lambelet's strange landscapes on the walls.

Up the bamboo staircase our visitor will find Mrs Fitzherbert's Room though, as we have seen, that good lady never lived in the Pavilion. The furniture, though, does come from her house which was nearby. Then we have two bedrooms, Princess Charlotte's and Queen Victoria's. From here we go on to Queen Charlotte's and then, down the stairs, to the King's Apartments. Here once again all is restored very much to what it was in 1821, with original wallpapers and mirrors and bookcases. From the anteroom our visitor goes through the noble Library to the Royal Bedroom. His tour is over.

Outside again we are left to quote the words of Dr Clifford Musgrave, the Royal Pavilion's inspired Director during the main period of its restoration:

> Perhaps the Pavilion's great purpose henceforth may be to serve as a perpetual reminder that no great epoch of civilisation has been without its vision of an ideal land, of a Golden Age . . .

In 1815 Nash had begun work on the building that was to be a vision of a Golden Age. One year later his contemporary, the poet Samuel Taylor Coleridge, opened his famous poem with the words:

In Xanadu did Kubla Khan a stately pleasure-dome decree.

Whatever the delays and disasters and the expense and extravagance of George IV's Royal Pavilion, it remains today an evocation of the poetic image surely as affecting and visionary as this.

Porte Cochère of the Pavilion

The Corridor and 'Bamboo' Staircase

The Corridor, also known as the Long or Chinese Gallery

The East Front of the Pavilion

The East Front of the Pavilion

'HRH The Prince Regent awakening the Spirit of Brighton'
Rex Whistler's Allegory, painted in 1944

The North Drawing Room

*One of the palm-tree columns, entwined with serpents, in the
North Drawing Room*

A corner of the Banqueting Room

The Banqueting Room today, showing the celebrated gasolier hanging from the plantain tree in the centre of the domed ceiling

The Banqueting Room at the time of the Prince Regent

The Music Room, photographed before the fire of November 2nd, 1975

The Music Room: the Prince Regent is on the left, seated between Lady Conyngham, his last mistress, and her daughter

The Riding House (now the Corn Exchange) in the time of the Prince Regent

The Great Kitchen

The Prince Regent's bed in the King's Apartments.